F.O.C.U.S.E.D

by Alainna Stephens

Heritage Publishing

ISBN: 979-8-9930373-0-1

F.O.C.U.S.E.D

Published by Heritage Publishing

ISBN: 979-8-9930373-0-1

Printed in the United States of America.

Contents of F.O.C.U.S.E.D.

F..C.U.S.E.D

Introduction

The Fight to Stay Focused

I didn't set out to write a book about focus.

I set out to survive a season where everything in my life felt like a distraction—some of it loud and obvious, and some of it quiet and convincing. Work pressures, spiritual burnout, emotional detours. I knew God had called me. I believed He had more for me. Yet I found myself constantly pulled away from what mattered most.

I was busy, Yet unfruitful. Present, Yet not aligned. Moving, Yet not progressing.

That's when I realized distraction doesn't always look like laziness or rebellion. Sometimes it looks like overcommitment, exhaustion, or spiritual autopilot.

God met me in the middle of that fog with one word: F.O.C.U.S.E.D. This book is the result of that journey. It's not a list of rules. It's not a guide to hustle culture.

It's a spiritual roadmap—for people who want to honor their assignment, protect their peace, and hear God clearly again.

If you've been feeling spiritually scattered, weary, or stuck, I get it.

Because when you are F.O.C.U.S.E.D., distractions lose their power, purpose comes into view, and your life becomes a testimony to what God can do with someone fully aligned with His will.

Why the Checkpoints Matter

Before we dive into the first chapter, I want to share something personal—something that shifted everything for me.

This book didn't come from a place of ease. It came from exhaustion. From pouring out so much that I forgot what it felt like to be poured into. From carrying burdens I didn't even realize I had picked up. From being in a constant cycle of doing for others while silently wondering who would help me refocus.

I remember sitting in a quiet room after a long day, completely drained. No music. No screens. Just me and God. And in that stillness, one word came to my spirit: F.O.C.U.S.E.D.

Not in a loud, commanding way—Yet like a whisper with weight. A whisper that carried a blueprint.

F.O.C.U.S.E.D

I started writing the word down, letter by letter. And with each letter, God revealed something deeper:

- **F** – Fix Your Eyes on the Father
- **O** – Obey Without Hesitation
- **C** – Cut Out the Clutter
- **U** – Understand the Assignment
- **S** – Stand Firm in the Spirit
- **E** – Expect the Promise
- **D** – Discipline Over Distraction

Each one became a checkpoint—not a checklist. Not something to master overnight. Yet a guide to help me re-center when life tried to pull me in every direction. A spiritual map for getting back on course when I felt lost, delayed, or just plain overwhelmed.

These chapters are more than themes. They're lived experiences. They are the waypoints I needed when I couldn't see clearly. And I believe they can serve you too—wherever you are right now.

So, take a deep breath.

You don't have to have it all figured out. You just have to take the first step.

Let's begin.

Chapter 1: F – Fix Your Eyes on the Father

"Let us fix our eyes on Jesus, the author and finisher of our faith..."— Hebrews 12:2 (NIV)

There is no focus without a focal point. And for the believer, that focal point must be God. Not the situation. Not the pressure. Not the detour or delay. When life pulls you in every direction, your posture must be one of spiritual re-centering—fixing your eyes on the Father.

This isn't about ignoring the chaos around you. It's about anchoring your spirit in the One who never moves. Focus, in its purest form, is about alignment. And there's no greater alignment than putting your gaze back on the One who created you, called you, and is carrying you.

The Danger of Distracted Vision

Distraction is one of the enemy's most subtle weapons. It doesn't always look like sin—it can look like busyness, overcommitment, or even a good opportunity that's not a God opportunity. A scattered mind produces a scattered life. If the enemy can't destroy you, he'll divide your attention until you lose sight of God's plan.

F.⊛.C.U.S.E.D

Peter walked on water—until he looked at the storm. His footing didn't fail. His focus did. The moment he shifted his eyes from Jesus to the waves, fear replaced faith, and he began to sink. (Matthew 14:29-30)

How often do we do the same?

When the marriage isn't working, the finances are tight, or the diagnosis feels too heavy, we instinctively start staring at the waves instead of the Savior.

Distracted vision is more dangerous than we realize. It doesn't always look like disobedience. Sometimes, it looks like misalignment disguised as opportunity. You're moving—Yet not toward what God called you to. You're producing—Yet not bearing lasting fruit. You're busy—Yet not building anything eternal.

When your vision is distracted, you start chasing what looks right instead of waiting on what is right. You begin to bend God's will to your preference. You stop asking "Is this God?" and start asking "Can I make this work?"

F..C.U.S.E.D

What pulls your vision eventually pulls your life.

Tyler Perry, one of the most influential creators in modern media, openly shares how a distracted vision nearly cost him his calling.

Early in his career, he faced rejection, homelessness, and failed stage plays. He doubted whether he was cut out for storytelling. In a moment of distraction, he considered abandoning faith-centered stories altogether to chase mainstream approval. He almost changed his entire creative focus—thinking it was the only way to succeed.

Yet after one of his lowest moments, he recounts sitting in silence and feeling a pull from God:

Don't change the message—just trust the process.

He shifted back to his original God-given vision. He stayed focused on creating content that lifted people spiritually, emotionally, and relationally. That refocus changed everything.

Today, his empire is built on the very thing he almost walked away from—because he recentered his vision on what God gave him, not what others demanded of him.

F..C.U.S.E.D

The Truth Is…

You can't walk in full purpose with partial focus.

God will never bless the version of your life you created to please people. Yet He will multiply the one you surrendered fully to Him.

Distraction delays destiny. Yet clarity restores power.

We live in a world that constantly pressures us to perform, conform, and impress. Social media has made it easier than ever to curate identities—to present versions of ourselves that are polished, palatable, and often filtered to fit what others expect.

Here's what it really comes down to:

God doesn't anoint who you pretend to be.

He blesses authenticity.

He breathes on surrender.

He multiplies what's yielded.

So many of us are stuck—It wasn't because we're lazy, It wasn't because we're unqualified—Yet because we're asking God to elevate a version of ourselves that He never authored. We're walking around carrying callings that were never ours. Saying yes to people and projects that dilute our purpose.

And the result?

Confusion. Burnout. Bitterness.

Because "clarity can't live where compromise reigns".

God is not obligated to bless the identity you built on fear, people-pleasing, or approval addiction. Yet the moment you release that false narrative and return to your original design—the you He formed before you were in your mother's womb—everything begins to shift.

Why? Because clarity restores power.

When you see God clearly, you begin to see yourself clearly. And when you see yourself clearly, you stop giving pieces of your destiny away in exchange for validation.

You don't need to perform for God. You need to present yourself to Him. And in doing so, He'll multiply what you were afraid to offer: your full, unfiltered, surrendered self.

Focus Requires Intentional Vision

Fixing your eyes on the Father is not a passive action—it's a deliberate, daily discipline. It's a choice you make before the noise of the day sets in, before circumstances try to distract you, before your emotions take the lead. It's deciding that no matter what comes your way—whether it's a celebration or a crisis—you will look to God first.

When you wake, you set your attention on Him before you set your feet on the floor. When doubt creeps in like a shadow, you lift your eyes to the Light that never dims. When decisions feel weighty and uncertain, you seek His face—not merely His hand—because you want His heart, not just His help.

Your focus becomes your filter, shaping the way you see the world around you. When your gaze is locked on the Father, the magnitude of fear shrinks in the light of His power. Peace is no longer elusive; it becomes a resting place you can enter at will. Wisdom stops being something you chase—it begins to flow into your spirit like a steady stream.

F.☙.C.U.S.E.D

And as your focus sharpens, so does your vision. Distractions lose their power. The enemy's tactics lose their sting. You begin to notice the subtle ways God has been guiding you all along. The fog lifts, and the path before you becomes clearer—It wasn't because the journey is suddenly easy, Yet because your sight is fixed on the One who knows the way.

Practices That Help You Stay Focused

• *Daily Time in the Word*: Scripture realigns your sight with truth. It silences the lies and distractions of the world.

• *Prayer and Meditation*: These aren't just rituals—they're recalibrations. They pull you out of your own head and back into God's presence.

• *Worship*: Worship shifts your gaze from the size of the problem to the size of your God.

• *Spiritual Accountability*: Stay connected to others who will remind you where to look when your vision drifts.

A Focused Life Bears Fruit

When your eyes are fixed on the Father, your heart inevitably follows. And when your heart follows, everything else in your life begins to align. From that place, your decisions are shaped by His wisdom, your relationships are nurtured with His love, and your responses to adversity reflect His peace rather than your panic.

A focused life isn't a life without battles—it's a life anchored in the unshakable truth that God is greater than every battle, bigger than every storm, and more faithful than every fear. It's the understanding that while trouble may visit your doorstep, it can't take up permanent residence in a heart that's rooted in Him.

As you walk this journey of becoming *F.O.C.U.S.E.D*, remember:

God never promised that distractions wouldn't come. He never promised the road would be without detours, delays, or difficulties. Yet He did promise that His presence would go with you—and that His presence would always be enough when they do. His presence is your compass in confusion, your shelter in chaos, your steady hand in the shaking.

So today, make the conscious choice to lift your eyes. Look up to the One who sees the end from the beginning. Look past what is temporary, and fix your gaze on what is eternal. Don't just glance at Him when it's convenient—lock your eyes on Him like a lifeline you refuse to let go.

The Father is not only where your focus begins—He is where your focus must remain. Because when you keep Him at the center, everything else finds its rightful place. And in that place, you'll discover the unexplainable peace, clarity, and strength to live with purpose no matter what comes.

Distraction: The Art of the Detour

Distractions don't always come in the form of sin. Sometimes, they show up as good things wrapped in the wrong timing. Sometimes, it's not a door God never opened—it's one He did, Yet you stayed in the hallway too long. Or you walked through it prematurely.

Distraction is sneaky like that. It's not always loud. It's not always evil. Yet it is always designed to do one thing—pull your attention away from God's path and promise.

That thing, that person, that habit, that feeling—you know what it is. It's the text you keep answering. The opportunity that glitters Yet doesn't grow you. The relationship that comforts your emotions Yet drains your spirit. The scrolling that soothes your boredom Yet steals your purpose. The lie that you're not ready, not good enough, not chosen.

F.O.C.U.S.E.D

We rarely get distracted by things we hate. Most distractions are dressed in something we enjoy. Something that feels familiar. Something that gives us just enough dopamine to keep us coming back for more—until we look up one day and realize we haven't moved in weeks.

We're stuck.

Paralyzed.

Off course.

And worst of all, numb to the presence of God because we've become overstimulated by everything else.

Navigating Distractions in the Physical Realm

Life will never be distraction-free. The question is: How do you move forward despite them?

The truth is:

Your focus will always cost you something, Yet so will your distraction.

To stay Fixed on the Father in a world designed to fracture your focus, you have to commit to intentional practices that protect your mind, heart, and spirit. It's not just about saying you want to focus—it's about structuring your life so that focus becomes your spiritual posture.

• **Recognize your patterns.**
Distraction rarely shows up in obvious ways—it's often woven into the habits and cycles we've learned to live with. Ask yourself: What keeps stealing my time and attention? Is it the comfort of avoiding what's hard? The fear of failing? The constant chase for validation? Until you name it, you can't confront it. God will often reveal the roots of distraction so you can address the real issue, not just its symptoms. Awareness is the first step toward freedom.

• **Set boundaries.**
Every "yes" to a distraction is an unspoken "no" to divine direction. That's why boundaries are not barriers—they're safeguards. Protect your focus like it's sacred—because it is. If the enemy can't destroy you, he'll try to distract you. That's why you must be willing to say no without guilt and yes without hesitation when God calls. Guard your time, guard your peace, and guard your assignment like a priceless treasure.

F..C.U.S.E.D

• Be spiritually honest.
There are seasons when we tell ourselves we're "waiting on God,"
when the truth is, we're just distracted by what we want more than
His will. That's not waiting—it's wandering. Spiritual honesty
requires you to ask: Am I truly seeking His plan, or am I stalling
because I don't like His answer? God can work with your honesty
far more than He can work with your pretense.

• Guard your gates.
Your eyes, your ears, and your mind are gateways to your spirit.
What you watch, who you listen to, and where you invest your
energy will either feed your faith or fuel your flesh. You can't
expect to have a mind of peace if you're constantly consuming
chaos. You can't expect to walk in clarity if you're allowing
confusion to speak into your life. Every gate you leave unguarded
becomes an entry point for distraction—so choose wisely what and
who you allow in.

Yet let's flip that.

God Is Always Showing—Yet Are You Willing to See?

God is moving. He never stopped. His hand is not idle, His voice is not silent, and His plans have not stalled. Even when the waiting feels empty. Even when the silence feels deafening. Even when your surroundings look nothing like the promise He spoke over your life—He is still working, still weaving, still aligning every detail for His glory and your good.

The problem is often not that God isn't showing—it's that we've trained our eyes to see only what we want to see. We filter His movement through the lens of our preference, rather than the lens of His purpose. If the path feels too hard, we assume it's not Him. If the timing feels too long, we assume He's forgotten. If the outcome doesn't match the one we scripted in our mind, we call it a closed door instead of a divine redirection.

Yet here's the thing—God doesn't bend His will to fit our expectations. He invites us to bend our will to fit His. And that means learning to see Him in the ways we didn't expect, at the times we didn't plan, and in places we didn't think to look.

Sometimes, what we call "a delay" is really His protection. Sometimes, what feels like "a detour" is actually His preparation. Sometimes, the "silence" is simply His way of sharpening your hearing.

The truth is, God is always showing—Yet are you willing to see Him outside the boundaries of your comfort? Are you willing to accept His version of the story, even when it looks nothing like yours? Are you willing to believe He's working even when you can't trace His hand?

Because when you shift your perspective from What do I want God to do? to What is God already doing?—you stop living in constant disappointment and start living in constant discovery. You begin to see that every step, every pause, and every pivot was Him guiding you all along.

Re-Centering Your Vision

This chapter is not about condemnation. It's about realignment. About returning your eyes to the Father—It wasn't because you've failed, Yet because He's still faithful.

You don't need to be perfect to be focused. You just need to be willing.

Willing to refocus.

Willing to release.

Willing to redirect your attention, daily, back to the One who sees beyond your now.

Let this be the day you decide to stop settling for distractions. Let this be the moment you clear the clutter and fix your eyes again. You may have looked away for a moment, Yet God never stopped looking at you.

When Fear Becomes the Distraction

Not all distractions are loud. Some whisper. Some come dressed in logic, practicality, or even wisdom. Yet one of the most crippling distractions you'll ever face is fear—especially fear of change.

It's easy to identify the obvious distractions. Yet fear? Fear can masquerade as caution. It can make you overthink an open door until it shuts. It can keep you planted in familiar soil even when God's trying to replant you for growth. Fear of leaving that job, starting that business, ending that relationship, or moving to that new place—it doesn't always feel like disobedience, Yet it delays the obedience God is calling you into.

You can be so used to a certain environment, even if it's stifling, that stepping out feels dangerous. Yet sometimes fear is not a warning—it's a test. A test to see if you'll move anyway. A test to see if you'll choose trust over terror.

Faith It Anyway

There are moments in your journey when the only strategy left is to clench your teeth and faith it. Not fake it—faith it.

That means:

• Moving even when your knees are shaking.

• Saying yes even when your voice is trembling.

• Letting go even when you have no visible safety net.

This isn't reckless—it's reverent. It's your soul's way of telling God, "I'm scared, Yet I trust You."

Fear is not always the enemy. Yet when it becomes your decision-maker, it becomes a distraction. It diverts your trajectory and delays your potential. And when fear becomes familiar, it starts to feel like truth—even when it's lying to you.

Trusting the Process (Even When It's Hard)

Trusting God's process isn't glamorous. It's not a neat, pretty progression from one mountaintop to another. It's detours. Delays. Dry places. And deep pruning. There are days when trusting God feels like walking blindfolded toward a cliff, believing a bridge will appear mid-step.

Yet it's in those places where your faith sharpens. Where your focus is forged. God often allows the discomfort not to punish you, Yet to prepare you. He's not trying to hurt you—He's trying to stretch you into the person He called you to be.

What looks like a setback might be a setup. What feels like silence might be God building your spiritual muscles behind the scenes. Faith isn't always about having no fear—it's about not letting fear have you.

The Decision to Move Forward Anyway

Choosing to move despite fear is one of the boldest expressions of faith. It sends a clear signal to Heaven:

"Lord, I'm terrified, Yet I believe You more than I believe what I see."

And that kind of faith gets God's attention. That kind of faith moves things in the unseen realm. It tears down spiritual walls. It brings alignment. It opens doors.

So ask yourself:

What fear is holding me back? What would I pursue if fear wasn't a factor? What is God asking me to step into that my comfort zone won't let me reach?

The fear you face may never fully disappear—Yet the courage to focus in spite of it is where transformation begins.

Prayer: When Fear Tries to Distract Me

Father God,
I come to You with an honest heart.
One that sometimes feels afraid—of change, of the unknown, of
stepping outside the safety of the familiar.
Yet today, I choose to fix my eyes on You.

Even when distractions surround me,
Even when fear whispers louder than faith,
Even when I can't see how it's all going to work out—
I trust that You are still in control.

Lord, help me to silence every voice that pulls me away from Your
promise.
Remind me that fear is not my guide—You are.
Give me the courage to move even when I don't have all the
answers.

Let every step I take in faith be a signal to Heaven that I believe
You over everything I see.

F.O.C.U.S.E.D

When the journey gets hard, be my strength.
When the process feels slow, be my patience.
When I feel alone, be my peace.

I don't want to bend Your will to fit my plans.
I want to surrender my plans to fit Your will.
Let my life be evidence that even through fear, I trusted You.
In Jesus' name, Amen.

F..C.U.S.E.D

Affirmation: I Am Focused

I fix my eyes on God, not my circumstances.

What I see around me will not shake what I know within me.

I am not led by fear—I am led by faith.

Even when I feel afraid, I move forward because I trust God's plan.

Distractions no longer dominate my life.

I recognize them, release them, and return my focus to the Father.

God is moving even when I can't feel Him.

I choose to believe beyond what I can see.

My focus is a form of worship.

Each moment I stay centered on God's purpose, I honor His presence.

I release my need to control the outcome.

I trust that God's timing is perfect and His promises are sure.

I will not craft a narrative to comfort my fears.

I will live the truth of God's word, even when it challenges me.

I am courageous. I am steady. I am aligned.

My steps are ordered, my heart is open, and my eyes are fixed on Him.

F..C.U.S.E.D

Life… is a journey.

And like any road, it comes with detours, speed limits, roadblocks, and stop signs.

Every piece of it is designed with purpose—Yet that doesn't always mean it feels that way.

There was a time I found myself on what felt like a roller coaster with no direction, or worse—a hamster wheel with no off-ramp. Spinning. Exhausted. Moving, Yet going nowhere.

I kept praying, "God, please… just give me a space in time to slow down, to be still."

I was doing all the "right" things:

• Going to church.

• Serving in ministry.

• Showing up for people.

• Pouring out wherever I could.

F.O.C.U.S.E.D

Yet somewhere in the middle of it all—I lost sight of the One I was supposed to be looking at.

I had a servant's heart, Yet my boundaries were broken.

I gave and gave… and eventually felt like I had nothing left.

I felt unfocused, overwhelmed, and honestly, confused.

It wasn't because I wasn't doing good things—Yet because I wasn't doing the things God had assigned for me in that moment.

Even good can become a distraction when it's unbalanced. I didn't know how to juggle everything.

I didn't feel like I was progressing. I was exhausted and didn't know how to ask for help—because I thought focus meant holding it all together.

Yet that's not what God asks of us. He never said, "Be everything to everyone." He said, "Fix Your Eyes On Me."

And when I finally slowed down—when I stopped trying to manage it all and simply sat in His presence—clarity returned.

Not all at once. Yet piece by piece, He began to center me again.

Because focus isn't about multitasking—it's about prioritizing.

And sometimes, the most spiritual thing you can do…
is recenter your gaze.

Chapter 2: O – Obey Without Hesitation

"To obey is better than sacrifice…"

— 1 Samuel 15:22 (NIV)

Obedience isn't always comfortable. In fact, it rarely is. Yet it is essential. God doesn't call us to understand before we act—He calls us to trust and move.

Obedience is not just about rules or restrictions—it's about relationship. It's your heart saying, "God, I trust Your voice more than I trust my own understanding."

Hesitation is often the gap where doubt grows. When God gives an instruction, delaying it can lead to disobedience—even if it's unintentional. The longer you wrestle with "if" or "when," the easier it becomes to question whether you heard Him at all.

True obedience requires surrender. And surrender requires faith.

Partial Obedience is Still Disobedience

We don't often say "no" to God. More often, we say "not yet," or "maybe later," or "I'll go, Yet not all the way." Yet God doesn't bless partial obedience. Delayed obedience is still disobedience.

Think of Jonah. God told him to go to Nineveh, Yet he ran in the opposite direction. It wasn't because he didn't hear God—Yet because he didn't like what God said. His disobedience didn't cancel God's call; it just complicated his path. The storm, the fish, the detour—all of it came It wasn't because Jonah was outside of his calling, Yet because he was outside of obedience.

How often do we do the same? We say we're waiting for a sign when, in truth, we're just unwilling to move without full control. We mask disobedience with delay. Yet purpose is activated through immediate obedience.

Obedience Isn't About Ease—It's About Trust

God doesn't call us to what's convenient. He calls us to
what's consecrated. Sometimes, the most uncomfortable step is the
most anointed one. Obedience may lead you into the wilderness,
Yet it will never lead you away from God's will.

When God told Abraham to sacrifice Isaac, the instruction made no
sense. It was the very promise God had given him—now He was
asking Abraham to lay it down. Yet Abraham obeyed. Without
hesitation. And because of his obedience, God provided what
Abraham could not see beforehand—a ram in the thicket. (Genesis
22)

Obedience often doesn't make sense until you see the provision on
the other side. Yet you don't get to see the miracle if you don't take
the step.

Why We Hesitate

• Fear of failure. What if I'm wrong? What if it doesn't work?

• Fear of loss. What will I have to give up?

• Fear of judgment. What will people think?

• Fear of discomfort. What if this hurts?

The truth is, every time you obey, Heaven backs you. You are not
stepping out alone. God never gives an instruction without
supplying the grace to follow it.

The issue is rarely God's clarity. It's our courage.

Obedience Is an Act of Worship

Saying yes to God is more than just compliance—it's intimacy. It's declaring, "I know You're good, even when I don't know where You're taking me." Every time you obey, you deepen your connection with the Father.

Obedience changes your posture. It sharpens your focus. It invites clarity and favor. It unlocks what delay keeps bound.

Ask Yourself:

• What is God asking me to do that I've been putting off?

• Where have I substituted comfort for calling?

• Have I confused delay for discernment?

The Call to Obey Without Hesitation

Let this be the moment you stop asking for confirmation for what God already told you to do. Let this be the chapter where you say yes, It wasn't because it's easy, Yet because it's right. Because your promise is on the other side of your obedience.

Don't wait for the full picture. Just obey.

F.O.C.U.S.E.D

When I Needed More Than a Nudge

Obedience isn't hard because we don't want to follow God—it's hard because we want to understand everything before we do.

I've been there.

There was a season when I felt God nudging me to leave a situation that had become draining. Not just tiring—Yet spiritually suffocating. I kept praying for clarity, for confirmation, for a sign. And God, in His mercy, kept showing me over and over what I needed to do.

Yet instead of moving, I stayed.

I rationalized. I told myself I was just being loyal… just being wise… just trying to finish what I started. Yet deep down?

I was scared.

Scared of starting over.

Scared of failing.

Scared that what was next wouldn't feel as safe—even if I wasn't really safe where I was.

And so I delayed. I paused. I hesitated. I disguised fear as faithfulness.

It wasn't until things became undeniably chaotic—circumstances I couldn't control, conversations that shook me, spiritual weight I couldn't lift—that I realized:

God wasn't waiting on me to understand. He was waiting on me to move.

Obedience Often Doesn't Make Sense Until You Move

Sometimes, you won't see the provision until you walk in the direction God has pointed. The breakthrough doesn't meet you at the beginning—it meets you in the movement. The miracle isn't always waiting where you are; it's waiting where you're willing to go.

I know this firsthand.

After more than 20 years in corporate America, I began to feel something shift inside me. What once felt purposeful now felt heavy. I wasn't just unfulfilled—I was burdened. Each day became more draining than the last. The joy was gone. The interest had faded. I started asking myself quietly, "Is this it? Is this all I'm meant to do?"

God, being the loving Father that He is, knew He couldn't whisper me out of that season—He had to shake me out of it. He knows me well enough to know I often need an in-my-face kind of clarity or I'll try to logic my way through discomfort, trying to fix what He never intended me to stay in.

The truth is—He allowed the chaos at work. Not to punish me, Yet to position me. Not to destroy me, Yet to deliver me. He was creating the disruption I wouldn't create for myself. And while I kept trying to make peace with a place He was trying to move me from, He kept whispering the same question to my spirit:

"Do you trust Me?"

It wasn't that I didn't believe God had more for me—I just didn't believe I was qualified for anything different. I had already built the narrative in my mind: This is all I know. This is all I've ever done. Yet God wasn't asking me to know—He was asking me to obey.

He had already qualified me for the next.

Now it was up to me to walk in faith.
And here's what I've learned:

When you know in your spirit that God is calling you to do something—even if it makes no sense—delaying becomes disobedience. Obedience is not just about doing it right; it's about doing it when He says to.

When I finally obeyed, peace came—It wasn't because the path was easy, Yet because the pressure lifted. The heaviness wasn't just from my situation—it was from resisting God's direction.

That situation taught me that sometimes, we don't need another nudge.

We need to say yes.

We need to move.

We need to trust that obedience unlocks things hesitation never will.

Prayer: When Obedience Feels Uncertain

Heavenly Father,

Thank You for speaking, even when I hesitate to listen.

Thank You for being patient with me as I wrestle between comfort and calling.

I confess that fear sometimes holds me back—

Fear of failing, of starting over, of not being enough.

Yet today, I choose to trust You.

It wasn't because I can see every step ahead,

Yet because I know You're already waiting in my next.

Help me not to delay obedience with overthinking.

Help me to release control and step forward in faith.

When the path is unfamiliar, remind me that You are familiar.

You go before me. You surround me. You qualify me.

F..C.U.S.E.D

So I silence the noise of doubt.

I ignore the voice of fear.

And I lean into Your instruction—even when I don't understand it.

Let my obedience be my worship.

Let my yes echo in Heaven.

And let my steps lead me into everything You've already prepared for me.

In Jesus' name, Amen.

Affirmation: I Obey Without Hesitation

I trust God's voice more than I trust my fears.

He will never lead me into anything He hasn't already prepared me for.

I don't delay when God directs.

Every time I obey, I align with His best for my life.

My obedience unlocks divine provision.

Even when I can't see the full picture, I take the step.

I am not limited by my past experience.

God has qualified me for my next—even when it looks unfamiliar.

Obedience is my act of worship.

I honor God by moving when He says move.

I let go of the need to understand everything.

I follow in faith, knowing He's in full control.

I will not bend God's will to fit my comfort.

I surrender fully, and I walk boldly into His plan for me.

Journal Reflection: Obedience in Motion

Use this space to reflect, release, and realign your heart with God's instructions. Be honest. Be vulnerable. Be open.

1. What is God currently asking me to do that I've been hesitant to obey? (This may be a decision, a conversation, a move, a career shift, or a spiritual discipline.):

2. What fear or belief is keeping me from saying "yes" without hesitation? (Write down the lies fear has told you—and then write the truth of what God says in response.):

3. Have I been trying to fix something God is trying to move me away from? (Is there an area in my life where I've confused comfort with calling?):

4. What would trusting God fully in this season look like?
(Describe what bold, obedient action could look like if fear wasn't
in the way.):

5. Write a declaration of surrender.

(In your own words, declare your willingness to obey—even when
it's uncomfortable.):

Chapter 3: C – Cut Out the Clutter

"Every branch in Me that does not bear fruit He takes away; and every branch that bears fruit He prunes, that it may bear more fruit."

— John 15:2 (NKJV)

There comes a moment in every faith walk when you must declutter—spiritually, emotionally, and mentally. If you're going to stay focused on the Father, if you're going to obey without hesitation, then you must also have the courage to cut out what doesn't serve your growth.

Clutter doesn't always look messy. Sometimes it looks comfortable. Sometimes it looks sentimental. Sometimes it even looks productive. Yet anything that is draining your spirit more than it's developing it must be evaluated—and possibly eliminated.

God's process of pruning is not punishment—it's preparation. It's how He makes room for more.

What Is Clutter?

Clutter is anything that takes up space in your life Yet doesn't bear fruit.

It might be:

• A relationship that pulls you out of alignment with your assignment.

• A habit that consumes your time Yet never feeds your soul.

• A mindset that clings to fear, bitterness, or insecurity.

• Even a good thing that no longer serves the current season you're in.

The danger of clutter is that it distracts you subtly. You keep saying "yes" to everything until there's no space left for what actually matters. You keep busy, Yet not blessed. You're moving, Yet not progressing.

Sometimes the enemy doesn't have to destroy your focus—he just has to distract it with excess.

The Spiritual Weight of "Too Much"

There is such a thing as too much. Too much noise. Too much comparison. Too much access. Too much pouring out and not enough filling up. You were never created to carry everything. You were created to carry what's assigned.

Even Jesus withdrew from the crowds. Even He made time to separate, to pray, to filter out the noise so He could remain in tune with the Father's will.

We often ask God to give us more—more opportunity, more clarity, more influence. Yet we rarely ask Him to help us let go of the things we're already holding that are keeping our hands full.

Pruning Is the Price of Progress

When God starts cutting things back, it may feel like loss—Yet it's actually love. He prunes what is dead, yes. Yet He also prunes what's still growing—if it's not aligned with your future.

You may be holding onto something simply because it worked in the last season. Yet that doesn't mean it belongs in this one.

Clutter isn't just about what's around you. Sometimes it's what's inside you:

• Old wounds that keep you guarded.

• Shame from past decisions.

• People-pleasing that makes it hard to say no.

Clearing clutter is about reclaiming spiritual clarity. And that clarity brings capacity—to hear God clearly, move freely, and grow deeply.

Ask Yourself:

• What have I outgrown that I'm still holding onto?

• What habits or routines fill my time Yet not my spirit?

• Who has access to me that no longer aligns with where God is leading me?

• What am I keeping out of obligation or fear of being misunderstood?

Letting Go Isn't Easy—Yet It's Necessary

One of the greatest barriers to obedience is our grip. We hold on. To people. To places. To plans. To our own sense of control. And the tighter we cling, the harder it becomes to move when God calls.

Letting go isn't easy. It feels like loss. It feels like surrendering the very things that make us feel secure. Yet the truth is, obedience will often require you to release what's good so God can place what's greater in your hands.

Think about the rich young ruler (Mark 10:17–22). He had status, wealth, and influence. By every human measure, he was successful. Yet when Jesus invited him into a life of radical obedience—"Sell what you own and follow Me"—he walked away sad. Why? Because his hands were full. He couldn't release what he loved, so he forfeited what he longed for.

We do the same. We pray for new doors while refusing to close the old ones. We ask for fresh anointing while clinging to expired assignments. We beg God for clarity Yet grip tightly to relationships, jobs, and identities He's already told us to release.

The truth is—obedience and attachment cannot coexist. You can't step fully into God's next if you're still holding pieces of your past.

Letting go is never easy, Yet it is necessary.

- Necessary for your growth. God can't stretch you if you're unwilling to move beyond what feels familiar.

- Necessary for your protection. What you call comfort may actually be the very thing crippling your calling.

- Necessary for your testimony. On the other side of release is a story of provision and breakthrough that you can't see until you move.

Letting go doesn't mean forgetting. It doesn't mean what you released wasn't valuable. It simply means you trust God with the outcome more than you trust yourself with the control.

I've learned that the pain of release is temporary, Yet the fruit of obedience is eternal.

When Abraham lifted Isaac onto the altar, the hardest part wasn't the sacrifice—it was the surrender. It was unclenching his grip on the very promise God had given him. And yet, in that moment of surrender, God showed up with supernatural provision.

And He'll do the same for you.

Obedience will sometimes feel like you're losing, Yet Heaven always sees it as planting. What you place on the altar doesn't vanish—it multiplies in God's timing.

When Clutter Is Manufactured

Sometimes clutter isn't just what we pick up—it's what others pile on. In my own journey, God used a workplace storm to open my eyes to this truth.

What began as a typical corporate role soon spiraled into chaos. I started noticing how my leader began assigning me multiple tasks—tasks designed not to grow me, Yet to saturate every ounce of my time and energy. Deadlines would fall on holidays or during PTO I had already communicated. Tasks overlapped. Priorities shifted without notice.

It wasn't productivity—it was strategy.

A system designed to overwhelm.

A setup meant to create failure on paper, even when excellence was still in my heart.

At first, I tried to manage it. I told myself I could handle it. I thought maybe I wasn't organizing well enough, or maybe I just needed to push harder. Yet in my spirit, I began to sense something deeper: this wasn't just mismanagement—it was manipulation. And God was allowing it. Not to crush me, Yet to clarify me.

He was showing me in no uncertain terms:

This isn't just a toxic work culture—it's clutter.

And it's time to clear it.

I realized that the clutter in that environment wasn't just stealing my focus. It was blocking my capacity. I couldn't even feel what God was stirring in me because I was constantly trying to prove I could handle what was never mine to carry.

God was revealing the truth:

I wasn't just burnt out.

I was overloaded by design—not divine design, Yet human sabotage.

Yet even in that, He was working. Orchestrating chaos to guide me out of captivity. Clearing space not just around me, Yet within me, so I could move boldly into what He had already established as my next.

F.O.C.U.S.E.D

Prayer: When it's Time to Clear the Clutter

Father God,

Thank You for showing me what no longer belongs.

Even when I couldn't see it at first, You were revealing the weights I was never meant to carry.

Help me release the noise, the pressure, and the expectations that keep me bound.

Give me discernment to recognize what's fruitful versus what's just familiar.

Help me to let go of what no longer aligns with Your purpose for me.

I confess—I've held onto some things out of fear.

Fear of what others will say.

Fear of what I'll lose.

Fear of starting over.

Yet I trust You more than I trust my comfort.

If You're calling me to release it, I believe You've already prepared something better.

Make space in my heart, my mind, and my life for more of You.

Today, I choose clarity over chaos.

Focus over clutter.

Faith over fear.

In Jesus' name, Amen.

Affirmation: I Clear the Clutter to Make Room for Purpose

I release what no longer aligns with God's assignment.

If it distracts me, drains me, or diminishes me, it's not for me.

I make space for growth by pruning with purpose.

Letting go is not loss—it's preparation.

I am not obligated to carry what God never gave me.

False responsibility is not my portion.

I honor my future by decluttering my present.

My calling requires capacity, and I protect it with focus.

I choose clarity over chaos.

Noise will not drown out God's voice in my life.

Even when it's hard, I trust the pruning process.

God only cuts what He intends to grow back stronger.

I am becoming lighter, clearer, and more aligned.

I cut out the clutter—because my next requires space to thrive.

F..C.U.S.E.D

Not all clutter is visible.

Some of the heaviest things I've carried have never been seen—only felt.

There was a time I was emotionally weighed down by things that looked noble on the surface. I was helping people, showing up, being the "strong one." I was doing the things I thought I was supposed to do—until the weight of it all started making me feel buried.

It wasn't because God had given me too much…

Yet because I had picked up too many things He never handed me.

I realized I was carrying emotional clutter:

• Taking responsibility for other people's healing.

• Trying to be everything for everyone.

• Measuring my worth by how needed I felt.

• Internalizing problems that weren't mine to solve.

At the time, it felt like service. Yet it was actually self-neglect.

And when I finally slowed down long enough to ask God, "Why does everything feel so heavy?", I didn't hear correction—I heard an invitation:

"Daughter, put it down. I never asked you to carry that."

That moment shifted me.

I had been praying for clarity… Yet first, God had to clear out the clutter in my spirit.

The guilt.

The perfectionism.

The pressure to perform.

And slowly, as I released what wasn't mine, I made space for what was: peace, joy, and permission to simply be—not just do.

That's what clutter does: it crowds out clarity.

And cutting it out isn't selfish—it's spiritual survival.

Chapter 4: U – Understand the Assignment

"Wisdom is the principal thing; therefore get wisdom: and with all thy getting get understanding."

— Proverbs 4:7 (KJV)

Focus is impossible without understanding.

How can you stay on track if you don't know where you're going—or why you're going?

One of the greatest distractions in life is confusion of purpose. And confusion often leads to wandering. You try to be everything to everyone, saying yes to anything that feels like motion. Yet motion without mission becomes chaos. You stay busy, Yet never fruitful. You stay in motion, Yet never in alignment.

To truly be focused, you must understand your assignment—your divine reason for being in this season, in this space, with your specific gifts, experiences, and voice.

Assignment vs. Achievement

Misplaced focus often comes from chasing achievement rather than stewarding assignment.

Understanding your assignment isn't about checking off goals or chasing titles. It's about being obedient to what God has called you to do—even when it doesn't match what others expect or what makes the most money or sense.

Assignment is divine. It doesn't always show up on résumés or align with degrees. It's often shaped through pain, failure, detours, and divine downloads. Your assignment is what remains when the applause fades. It's what stirs your spirit when everything else feels still.

Why We Confuse the Two

Many of us mistake achievement for assignment. We reach for status, platforms, or accolades, thinking that's the mark of success. Yet spiritual success is measured in obedience, not optics.

- Achievement is about recognition. Assignment is about responsibility.

- Achievement is about what you collect. Assignment is about what you contribute.

- Achievement is about building your name. Assignment is about lifting His name.

The danger in chasing achievement is that it never satisfies. The goalpost keeps moving, the applause eventually fades, and the reward is fleeting. Yet when you walk in your assignment, there's a sustaining grace that carries you—even when no one else notices.

Biblical Examples

- Nehemiah's Assignment: He wasn't a priest or prophet; he was a builder. His assignment was to rebuild the walls of Jerusalem. By worldly standards, laying bricks didn't compare to holding a throne. Yet in God's economy, his obedience secured a nation.

- Moses' Assignment: He wasn't asked to build monuments or empires. His assignment was to lead people into freedom. The achievement wasn't in the miracles—it was in his obedience to keep saying "yes" to God's call.

- Jesus' Assignment: By human standards, He didn't achieve wealth, status, or political power. Yet He fulfilled the greatest assignment of all: redemption.

A Personal Lens

Ask yourself: Am I chasing what looks successful, or am I stewarding what God has assigned to me?
Your assignment may not trend on social media. It may not earn you the loudest applause. Yet it will bear eternal fruit.

I've learned that achievement can impress people, Yet assignment transforms lives. Achievement can fill a résumé, Yet assignment fulfills your soul.

Reflection Questions

- What am I currently pursuing—an achievement or an assignment?

- Do I measure success by recognition or by obedience?

- What has God whispered to me that may never make sense on paper Yet stirs something deep in my spirit?

When you choose assignment over achievement, you stop striving for validation and start living for significance.

Your Assignment Will Always Cost You Something

It may cost you your comfort.

It may cost you approval.

It may even cost you relationships that only understood the older version of you.

Yet it will always produce eternal fruit.

God doesn't give assignments to the most perfect or polished. He gives them to the willing. The ones who say, "God, I may not feel ready, Yet I trust that You are."

Understanding your assignment requires:

• **Self-examination**: What keeps coming back to your heart no matter how much you try to ignore it?

• **Spiritual discernment**: What has God been highlighting repeatedly in this season?

• **Bold surrender**: Are you willing to let go of what you wanted so you can embrace what He wants?

God Reveals Assignment Through Alignment

You don't have to chase your assignment. It will find you when you stay aligned with God's will. When you remain in His presence, in His Word, and in tune with His Spirit, your assignment will become unmistakably clear—even if it feels uncomfortable or unconventional.

He will confirm it through opportunities, through divine nudges, through others speaking what your spirit already knew. And sometimes, He'll confirm it by removing everything that no longer aligns so you finally stop fighting and start listening.

What Understanding Brings

• **Clarity of purpose** – You no longer waste time trying to be who you're not.

• **Authority** – You walk boldly in your lane without competing or comparing.

• **Endurance** – When things get hard, you don't quit—you remember your why.

• **Protection** – Understanding your assignment keeps you from distractions that look good Yet don't fit.

You don't have to understand the whole plan.

You just need to understand your part in it.

Ask Yourself:

• What makes me come alive spiritually?

• What problem am I uniquely gifted to help solve?

• What have I experienced that might now serve as fuel for my assignment?

• Have I allowed others' opinions or expectations to shape my direction more than God's voice?

Understanding releases the pressure. Once you truly understand your assignment, the need to prove yourself fades. You stop striving and start stewarding. You're no longer exhausted by trying to do everything—because you've locked in on the one thing God has called you to do.

And when you stay in your assignment, favor follows.

When the Holy Spirit Confirms the Assignment

Someone once told me, "What's understood doesn't need to be said." And it resonated deeply.

There's a kind of certainty that can't be explained—it can only be felt. That feeling? That knowing? That's the Holy Spirit. He is the divine translator between Heaven and your heart. He doesn't always speak in full sentences or clear instructions. Sometimes He just brings a settledness. A peace that surpasses understanding. A fire that won't burn out. A gentle push that says, "This is it."

The Holy Spirit is God's way of activating certainty in your spirit—long before things make sense on paper. He is the agent of understanding. He helps you recognize what's for you, even when it's unfamiliar. He helps you say yes to what aligns, and no to what distracts, without needing full explanation.

When the Holy Spirit confirms your assignment, it's not always loud. Yet it is always sure.

It's the reason you can walk away from a job, a role, or a title without regret.

It's why you can say no to what everyone else is running toward.

It's why you can endure seasons of obscurity—because you know God is building something eternal.

When He activates that understanding within you, it anchors you.

This is how you know it's God:

• It settles your spirit.

• It awakens your purpose.

• It doesn't always require words—because it's already written in your spirit.

When the Holy Spirit confirms something, you don't have to convince anyone else.

You just have to obey.

F..C.U.S.E.D

There's a strange comfort in doing what you're good at—even when your soul no longer feels aligned with it.

I've spent years excelling in a particular field. I had experience. I had the network. I had the resume that made sense. And for a long time, I told myself that because I was capable in it, I must also be called to it.

Yet deep down, I started to feel that internal tug—the kind that's quiet at first Yet becomes harder to ignore with time. The job wasn't fulfilling me anymore. The environment wasn't feeding me spiritually. I was performing—Yet I wasn't progressing.

At first, I brushed it off as burnout. I thought maybe I just needed a vacation or better boundaries.

Yet the truth was this:

I had outgrown what I was never meant to stay in.

And the more I clung to it, the more I confused achievement with assignment.

The turning point came when I realized I had been praying for God to give me direction—when He had already given it. I just didn't want to follow it, because it required me to walk into unfamiliar territory. A new chapter. A new calling. One that felt bigger than me.

And that's when I understood:

The assignment isn't always what's easy.

It's not always what pays the most.

It's not always what's popular or praised.

Yet it is always what's anointed.

The moment I surrendered to that truth, peace came. Clarity came. The pressure to perform faded, and a deeper hunger to walk in purpose took over.

God didn't create me to be impressive—He created me to be obedient.

And my assignment isn't found in applause.

It's found in alignment.

Prayer: When I Need Clarity and Alignment

Father God,

Thank You for creating me with intention.

You didn't make me to drift—you designed me with divine purpose.

In moments where I feel unclear or unworthy, remind me that You don't call the qualified—You qualify the called.

Holy Spirit, activate understanding in me.

Quiet the noise of the world and the voices of doubt.

Help me to hear You clearly, and to feel that deep certainty only You can provide.

Where I've confused busy with fruitful—realign me.

Where I've lost sight of my assignment—redirect me.

Where I've chased applause more than obedience—forgive me I don't want to build my life around assumptions or achievements.

I want to build it around assignment.

Even when I don't see the full path, help me walk with confidence in my part.

Give me the courage to obey, the wisdom to discern,

And the peace to stay planted where You've called me—until You call me forward again.

In Jesus' Name,

Amen.

Affirmation: I Understand My Assignment

I am created with divine purpose.

God doesn't make accidents—He makes assignments.

The Holy Spirit reveals what I need to know.

I don't need to chase clarity—God will confirm what's meant for me.

I no longer confuse activity with assignment.

I choose fruitfulness over busyness, calling over chaos.

Even if I don't know the whole plan, I trust the next step.

God's peace is my confirmation, and His Spirit is my guide.

I don't need outside approval for my divine assignment.

When Heaven affirms me, I don't need validation from man.

What's understood in my spirit doesn't always need to be explained.

When God speaks, I listen—and I move.

My focus is sharpened by understanding.

I walk in clarity, covered by grace, and aligned with purpose.

F.O.C.U.S.E.D

Journal Reflection: Understanding My Assignment

Use the space below to reflect deeply and listen to what the Holy Spirit might be revealing to you in this season.

1. What has God been consistently showing or confirming to me about my assignment in this season?

2. In what ways have I confused achievement or busyness with my true calling?

3. What have I felt deep within me that I've been hesitant to fully embrace? (A gift, a calling, a shift, a bold move?)

4. Where do I feel the Holy Spirit bringing peace, even if it doesn't fully make sense?

5. Write a declaration of alignment. (In your own words, declare your desire to walk boldly and faithfully in your assignment.)

Chapter 5: S – Stand Firm in the Spirit

"Therefore, take up the full armor of God, so that when the day of evil comes, you may be able to stand your ground…"

— Ephesians 6:13 (NIV)

What do you do when life starts to feel like sinking sand? When your footing slips? When the promise feels far and your faith feels fragile?

You stand.

Not in your strength.

Not in your plans.

Not in your emotions.

Yet in the Spirit.

Because standing firm in the Spirit isn't about confidence in your ability—it's about trust in His.

Standing Still Doesn't Mean Doing Nothing

We often confuse stillness with stagnation. Yet spiritually, standing firm is one of the most active postures you can take. It means refusing to be moved by what you see. It means choosing truth over trends. It means anchoring yourself in what God said, even when your world is screaming something else.

Standing still doesn't mean you're idle—it means you're intentional. It's the discipline of holding your ground while God fights battles you cannot. It's the maturity of choosing faith over frenzy. It's the wisdom of knowing that if God hasn't told you to move, your safest position is in His presence.

The Hard Reality of Stillness

Yet let's be honest—it's hard.

- Sometimes the storm feels louder than the Spirit.

- Sometimes we ask God for clarity, Yet all we hear is silence.

- Sometimes we're so tangled in our own thoughts, we can't tell if it's the Holy Spirit or just our own conscience echoing back our fears.

And when that happens, we do what most humans do:

We doubt.

We spiral.

We ask for a sign.

Stillness is not passivity—it's posture. It's standing in the gap between God's promise and its manifestation with unwavering faith. Exodus 14:13 reminds us of Moses' words to the Israelites: "Do not be afraid. Stand firm and you will see the deliverance the Lord will bring you today." They weren't told to build a bridge or swim across the Red Sea. They were told to stand still—and God parted the waters.

Stillness is not inactivity. It's active trust.

- Your worship in the waiting is warfare.

- Your prayer in the silence is progress.

- Your refusal to compromise is victory.

When you stand still, you are declaring with your posture: "My faith is not dependent on movement. My confidence is in the God who never changes."

Strength Training for the Soul

Think of stillness like strength training. Athletes often practice holding positions that burn muscles, It wasn't because it looks impressive, Yet because it builds endurance. Spiritually, standing still builds endurance in your faith. It teaches you to trust God's timing, sharpen your discernment, and resist the urge to manufacture answers He hasn't given.

Just like an athlete holding a plank, a wall-sit, or a weighted stance, the value isn't in how it looks—it's in what it produces. It doesn't look flashy. It doesn't post well on Instagram. Yet in that quiet, hidden discipline, strength is being forged that will carry you through the visible battles.

What God Builds in Stillness

When you stand firm, God is working muscles in you that quick victories never could:

The Muscle of Trust. Every second of waiting teaches your heart that God's plan is worth more than your timeline.

The Muscle of Discernment. Stillness sharpens your spiritual ears. Noise fades, and you learn the difference between His whisper and your worry.

The Muscle of Endurance. Every day you refuse to quit, you're training for the marathon of faith, not the sprint of emotion.

The Muscle of Humility. Stillness reminds you that it's not your striving Yet His strength that wins the battle.

The Holy Pause. Sometimes the holiest thing you can do is resist the urge to run ahead. Abraham and Sarah learned this the hard way when they tried to manufacture God's promise with Hagar (Genesis 16). Their impatience created complications that echoed for generations. The lesson? Waiting doesn't weaken the promise—it protects it.

When Stillness Feels Heavy

It's not easy to hold the weight of stillness. Muscles tremble. Doubt whispers. The urge to do something becomes overwhelming. Your mind starts replaying every scenario, wondering if you should've acted sooner, spoken up louder, or tried harder. Silence feels like failure. Delay feels like denial.

Yet here's the paradox: it's in that very tension that transformation takes place. Just like a muscle tears under resistance and rebuilds stronger, your faith stretches and matures in the seasons where nothing seems to be moving. Growth doesn't always happen in the rush forward—it happens in the quiet, hidden work of waiting.

Think of Joseph in prison. Forgotten by the cupbearer, unseen by men, Yet not forgotten by God. Those years of stillness were not wasted years—they were weight-training years. God was building the resilience Joseph would need to rule Egypt with wisdom, humility, and endurance.

F.☘.C.U.S.E.D

Think of the disciples between the crucifixion and the resurrection. The stillness of those three days must have felt unbearable—confusion, fear, grief. And yet, while they wrestled in silence, Heaven was orchestrating the greatest victory of all time. The pause wasn't empty. It was purposeful.

Stillness is never wasted when it's surrendered to God.

The Weight of Silence

Stillness feels heavy because it requires surrender. It strips away our illusions of control. It forces us to face the truth that we cannot manipulate God into moving faster, nor can we manufacture His promises with our own hands. In silence, every hidden fear rises to the surface, demanding to be confronted.

- What if nothing changes?
- What if I missed my chance?
- What if God forgot about me?

Yet in that confrontation, strength is born. Faith is not proven when everything is loud and obvious—it's proven when all you have is a whisper and you choose to cling to it anyway.

The Beauty of Renewal

Isaiah 40:31 says: "Yet those who wait on the Lord shall renew their strength; they shall mount up with wings like eagles; they shall run and not be weary, they shall walk and not faint." Notice the order—strength comes in the waiting, not the rushing. Renewal isn't about God finally catching up to your desires; it's about you catching up to His rhythm.

Eagles don't constantly flap their wings. They soar because they've learned how to ride the wind. Stillness positions you to catch the wind of God's Spirit, so when He moves, you don't exhaust yourself—you rise with Him.

The Quiet Work of God

While you wait, God is not idle. He is aligning people, places, and opportunities. He is shaping your heart, stretching your patience, and deepening your reliance on Him. Just because you don't see it doesn't mean He isn't doing it. The roots of a tree grow deepest in seasons unseen.

Sometimes, the greatest act of faith is simply holding your ground when everything in you wants to run ahead.

It's not easy to hold the weight of stillness. Muscles tremble. Doubt whispers. The urge to "do something" becomes overwhelming. Yet it's in that tension that transformation takes place. Just like a muscle tears and rebuilds stronger, your faith stretches and matures in the seasons where nothing seems to be moving.

Reflection Questions:

- Where is God asking me to stand still instead of strive?
- Am I mistaking His silence for absence?
- What "muscles" is God strengthening in me during this season? Trust? Endurance? Humility?
- How can I shift my perspective so that waiting feels like training, not punishment?

F.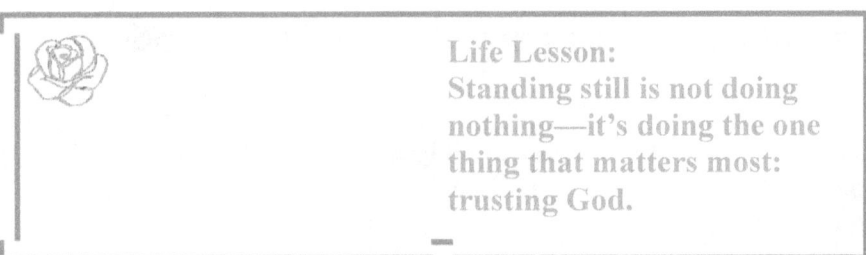.C.U.S.E.D

When You Don't Know if It's God or You

There are moments when I just need to ask, "Lord, is this You… or is it me?"

Is it the Holy Spirit speaking—or is it my desire disguised as discernment? Is it conviction—or just conscience? And if God hasn't given me the spirit of fear, why does fear sometimes feel so familiar?

Standing firm doesn't mean I never question—it means I keep believing even when I question.

It means I pray not just for answers, Yet for alignment.

I ask God to confirm it in a way I can't deny. To block what's not Him and breathe on what is.

And sometimes, I have to admit:

I get in my own way.

I overthink. I overcomplicate. I operate from trauma or pride or preference.

Yet the Spirit? He waits. He guides. He confirms.

So I ask Him daily—"Show me where I'm resisting Your leading. Help me trust what I know in my spirit more than what I feel in my flesh."

Standing Firm Doesn't Always Feel Good

There's a kind of strength that only develops when you don't move. When you stay planted, even when things look like they're falling apart.

And truthfully, there are things in me that are so strong—so certain—it would take a direct move of God to change them. That's how standing firm in the Spirit should be.

Yet standing firm doesn't mean standing alone.

It means standing with God's Word as your foundation.

Standing with the Spirit as your strength.

Standing with peace—even when your heart is pounding.

How to Stand Firm in the Spirit

• Cling to what God already said. Don't abandon truth for temporary relief.

• Pray for spiritual sensitivity. Ask God to help you distinguish between His Spirit and your own thoughts.

• Test the fruit. Is what you're sensing producing peace, humility, alignment with Scripture?

• Allow time to clarify. Sometimes, what feels unclear today becomes unmistakable tomorrow.

• Speak the Word aloud. Declare it until it becomes louder than your fear.

Ask Yourself:

• Where do I feel shaky right now—and what truth do I need to anchor myself in?

• Am I asking God to speak, Yet not giving Him space to answer?

• What patterns of fear or doubt do I need to release so I can stand in faith?

Standing Is a Form of Worship

When you refuse to be moved by doubt, fear, or disappointment—
you're declaring that God is still worthy of your trust. That's
worship. That's warfare. That's what it means to stand firm in the
Spirit.

Even when you're tired.

Even when it hurts.

Even when the outcome is unclear.

You stand—because you know Who's holding you up.

Standing firm isn't just a command—it's a design. God created us
to stand. From the moment a child takes their first steps, standing
is celebrated as a symbol of growth, development, and readiness
for movement. And just like in the physical, there are spiritual
benefits to standing.

Let's think about what happens when we stand—naturally and
spiritually.

Standing Builds Strength

In the physical body, standing builds leg strength. It activates the core. It engages the muscles required to keep you upright and balanced. Over time, standing makes you stronger—not just for the moment, Yet for the movement to come.

Spiritually, standing in the midst of hardship, uncertainty, or silence strengthens your faith muscles. Every time you refuse to quit, your endurance increases. Every time you stand when it would be easier to fold, your spiritual frame becomes more resilient. You begin to recognize that your ability to stand comes not from you—Yet from God holding you up.

Standing Improves Posture

When you stand up straight, your body realigns. Your head lifts. Your spine stacks properly. Your lungs open. Good posture allows you to breathe deeper and function better.

The same is true in the Spirit. Standing firm realigns your posture before God. It lifts your head when life tries to weigh you down. It causes you to breathe again—to stop hunching over in anxiety or shrinking back in fear. It reminds you who you are and Whose you are.

Standing Enhances Mental Well-Being

Research shows that physically standing—even just for a few minutes—can boost mental clarity, increase alertness, and reset emotional overwhelm. Why? Because standing wakes up your system. It shifts your perspective.

Spiritually, standing does the same. It centers your focus. It tells your mind, "We're not giving up." It signals to the enemy, "I may be attacked, Yet I'm not retreating."

When you choose to stand—especially in worship, prayer, or faith—you are renewing your mind and reminding your soul that victory is already promised.

F.@.C.U.S.E.D

God Designed You to Stand

Standing, if you have the physical ability, is something you
do organically every day. You don't overthink it. You just do it.
Why? Because God built it into your design.

Likewise, God has wired your spirit with the capacity to stand in
Him—to remain grounded in His Word, His will, and His presence.
He does all things with purpose, including giving you spiritual legs
to walk by faith and stand when life tries to knock you down.

Every time you stand in obedience…

Every time you stand in worship…

Every time you stand in truth when lies are louder—

You are worshiping God with your posture, not just your praise.

When Everything Felt Like Sinking Sand

There was a time in my life where I felt like everything beneath me was shifting.

Emotionally. Mentally. Spiritually.

I couldn't tell where the ground ended and the storm began.

Everything felt like sinking sand.

I was doing everything I knew to do—praying, serving, showing up—Yet nothing felt secure. I couldn't feel God the way I used to. I couldn't hear Him with the clarity I'd relied on in past seasons. The silence was deafening, and I started asking myself, Is this me?

Or is this God?

I wrestled with doubt.

I second-guessed every decision.

I prayed for a sign—any sign—that I was still on the right path.

Yet in the stillness, God didn't give me a full plan. He gave me a word:

"Stand."

I wanted relief. He gave me resilience.

I wanted an exit. He gave me endurance.

And slowly, I began to see that standing wasn't about feeling strong—it was about being grounded in what I knew was true. I had to stop trusting how I felt and start trusting what He said.

F.☙.C.U.S.E.D

The truth is, there are things I've believed for so long—deep convictions, spiritual truths—that I know would take a literal move of God to change. That's how firm I've had to learn to stand in the Spirit.

It doesn't mean I don't question.

It doesn't mean I don't feel fear.

It means I plant my feet anyway.

Standing firm, for me, became a form of worship.

It was the spiritual way of saying, "God, I don't understand it. Yet I'm not moving. Not until You say so."

Because when everything is shaking, the safest place to be—is anchored in Him.

Prayer: When I Feel Like I'm on Sinking Sand

Father God,

Sometimes I feel like the ground beneath me is giving way.

Like everything I knew is shifting. Like I'm standing in uncertainty, doubt, fear.

Yet today, I choose to plant my feet in You.

You are my firm foundation.

You are my unshakable Rock.

You are the one who strengthens me to stand—even when I feel like falling.

Forgive me for the times I've let fear speak louder than faith.

For the moments I've leaned on my own understanding more than Your Spirit.

Teach me to recognize Your voice—not just with my ears, Yet with my spirit.

Confirm what I need to know, and give me the peace to wait when You're silent.

F.O.C.U.S.E.D

Holy Spirit, help me to get out of my own way.

Silence my overthinking.

Clear the clutter of my conscience.

And let the truth of Your presence rise above all doubt.

When I feel weak, remind me that standing is worship.

That every moment I choose not to give up—I'm honoring You.

Strengthen me. Align me. Keep me grounded in Your truth.

In Jesus' name, Amen.

Affirmation: I Stand Firm in the Spirit

I am rooted in God's truth, not shaken by circumstances.

Even when life feels uncertain, my spirit stands firm.

I was created to stand.

God designed me with the strength to endure, the posture to worship, and the clarity to discern.

I don't stand alone—He holds me up.

His Spirit is my anchor, and His Word is my foundation.

I choose faith over fear.

I will not be moved by emotions or distractions.

Standing is my worship.

It realigns my posture, strengthens my resolve, and honors the God who never fails me.

Even in silence, I trust the Spirit's presence.

If I can't hear Him clearly, I will stand still until He speaks.

I am strong, steady, and spiritually grounded.

No matter what comes—I stand.

F.O.C.U.S.E.D

Journal Reflection: Standing in the Storm

Use this space to examine where you are being called to stand firm, and what God may be developing in you through this season of spiritual endurance.

1. Where in my life do I feel like I'm standing on sinking sand? (Be honest about the areas that feel unstable—emotionally, mentally, spiritually.)

2. What does "standing firm in the Spirit" look like for me right now? (Describe what spiritual posture, stillness, or faithfulness might look like in this season.)

3. Am I confusing my conscience or desires with the Holy Spirit's voice?(Ask God to help you discern clearly, and write what you feel prompted to release or realign.)

4. What truth from God's Word can I stand on this week? (Choose a scripture to anchor your focus and declare over your life.)

5. Write a declaration of strength. (In your own words, declare your intent to stand firm and trust the Spirit's guidance.)

Chapter 6: E – Expect the Promise

"Let us hold unswervingly to the hope we profess, for He who promised is faithful."

— Hebrews 10:23 (NIV)

Expectation is the posture of faith.

To expect something means you believe it's already in motion, even when you don't yet see the results. It's not wishful thinking—it's spiritual confidence rooted in the unchanging character of God.

Expectation is like leaning forward in your spirit. It's the posture of someone who knows a train is coming, even before they see the light on the tracks. They stand at the station ready, It wasn't because they've seen it yet, Yet because they trust the schedule.

When you're truly focused, you don't just work hard—you wait well. You keep showing up, standing firm, and obeying, even when the promise feels far away. Expectation anchors your soul while your circumstances catch up with what God already declared over your life.

Expectation Is Spiritual Vision

You may not be able to see the promise physically, Yet expectation sharpens your spiritual vision. It trains you to look beyond what is visible and lean into what is eternal. As Paul wrote, "For we walk by faith, not by sight" (2 Corinthians 5:7).

Expectation reminds you:

- God is not slow—He's strategic. His delays are designs, not denials.

- Delayed doesn't mean denied. The gap between the prayer and the promise is often where preparation happens.

- Just because it hasn't happened yet doesn't mean it's not already on the way. Daniel's prayer was answered the first day he prayed, Yet the angel was delayed for 21 days in the heavenly realm (Daniel 10:12–13). The unseen doesn't mean the undone.

God honors expectation that is rooted in faith. Because faith expects. Faith doesn't just believe God can—it lives like He will.

The Enemy Attacks Expectation First

The enemy knows he can't steal your promise, so he targets your posture. If he can weaken your expectation, he can drain your endurance. He doesn't have to destroy your faith—he just has to discourage it.

He whispers:

- "You're behind."

- "It's never going to happen."

- "God forgot about you."

And before you know it, your focus shifts:

- From anticipation to apathy.

- From praying boldly to barely speaking to God at all.

- From waking up with vision to simply surviving the day.

Yet The truth is,: God never asks you to manufacture the outcome—He asks you to maintain the expectation. You don't have to force open doors. You don't have to manipulate timelines. Your responsibility is faithfulness; His responsibility is fulfillment.

Holding Expectation in Tension

Expectation isn't easy. It's holding on in the middle. It's praying when the heavens feel brass. It's praising when your bank account is empty. It's sowing seeds when the ground still looks barren. Expectation is costly because it requires your heart to stay soft when disappointment wants to harden it.

Yet remember: the woman with the issue of blood pressed through the crowd because she expected healing if she touched Jesus' garment (Mark 5:28). The centurion shocked Jesus with his faith because he expected His word alone would heal his servant (Matthew 8:8–10). Expectation became the doorway for miracles.

Life Lesson:
Expectation is not passive—it's posture. It positions you to recognize and receive what God is already doing.

Waiting Is Not Wasted

There's a sacred tension in the waiting.

You've obeyed. You've stood firm. And now… you wait.

Not passively, Yet purposefully.

Sometimes the promise isn't being delayed—

you're being developed.

And development takes time.

Think about what it takes to develop anything of value—growth, skill, wisdom, character. It all requires intentional stages. Nothing fully formed emerges without a process. God doesn't rush what He's refining.

Waiting is where He tests your endurance, shapes your trust, strengthens your focus, and reveals what you still depend on outside of Him.

That discomfort you feel? That's by design.

Because comfort doesn't create capacity—pressure does.

This is the weight in the wait.

The invisible heaviness you carry when you're expecting something that hasn't arrived yet.

It's stretching you for what's ahead, not punishing you for where you are.

In many cases, the delay is for your safety. God knows what premature exposure can cost.

A rushed blessing may impress others, Yet a refined promise will sustain you. Prematurely developed things are often unstable, unreliable, or prone to malfunction. And God loves you too much to let you walk into something that looks like a blessing Yet functions like a burden.

So what feels like delay may actually be:

• An audit of your foundation

• A course correction for your character

• Or a pause that protects you from what you can't yet see

In the development process, you don't just wait on the promise—

you become the person who can carry it.

How to Expect Well:

• **Speak the Promise Daily**. Don't just hope for it—declare it.

• **Visualize the Outcome**. See yourself walking in what God spoke.

• **Prepare Like It's Coming**. Pack for the move. Build the business plan. Write the vision.

• **Praise in Advance**. Worship is your weapon while you wait.

• **Stay in Position**. Don't abandon your post because it hasn't arrived. Stay aligned.

Ask Yourself:

• Have I stopped expecting because I haven't seen results?

• What promise has God made that I've quietly given up on?

• Am I preparing for the outcome I'm praying for?

Expectation Is an Act of Worship

It says, "God, I believe You even when nothing looks like what You said."

It's hope, standing tall. It's focus, rooted deep. It's the spiritual discipline of living like what God promised is already yours.

Don't let time rob you of trust.

Don't let delay distract you from destiny.

The promise is still active.

And your expectation is the soil that gives it room to grow.

When the Promise Felt Personal... Yet So Did the Pain

I've always believed God had something big for me.

A calling. A gift. A promise. Something that wasn't just for me—Yet meant to impact others.

Yet somewhere in the waiting... doubt crept in.

Not the loud kind, Yet the subtle kind—the kind the enemy specializes in.

The kind that doesn't scream "give up," Yet whispers "you're not enough."

The devil began to chip away at my confidence—not just in the promise, Yet in me.

He tried to convince me that what I carried wasn't worthy.

That I was too late.

Too flawed.

Too small.

Too overlooked.

And I started asking God, "Why does it seem like everyone else gets a stage, a moment, a breakthrough... and I'm still in the shadows?"

It felt like I was being judged before I even had a chance to show what I could really do.

F.❀.C.U.S.E.D

Like people made assumptions about my potential without ever witnessing my passion.

And deep inside, I started to echo a question I was ashamed to admit:

When will it be my turn?

It didn't come from envy—it came from exhaustion.

I knew I was gifted. I knew I was called. Yet I was growing tired of watching the promise unfold for everyone else while I was still waiting for my release.

Yet here's what God showed me:

The delay isn't a dismissal—it's development.

The shadows aren't punishment—they're protection.

And the silence doesn't mean I'm forgotten—it means God is still writing the stage that's big enough for what He put inside me.

He reminded me that my gifts aren't inadequate.

They're just not for everyone's approval—they're for His glory.

And when it's my time, it will not only make sense… it will make impact.

So I stopped asking "when?"

And I started asking, "How can I stay faithful until then?"

Because I don't want the promise before I'm ready.

And I don't want the platform without His presence.

I want what's mine—in His time.

Prayer: When I'm Waiting and Weighed Down

Father God,

Thank You for the promise—

Even when I can't see it, feel it, or explain it.

Even when the wait feels heavy and the timeline doesn't make sense.

You are not slow—You are strategic.

You don't delay to hurt me—You develop me to prepare me.

Help me to trust that this process has purpose.

Even when I feel like I'm standing still, You're still moving.

Even when the door hasn't opened, You're still working behind the scenes.

I confess—I get tired.

I get discouraged.

I wonder if I misheard You.

I wonder if I did something wrong.

Yet I release all of that right now.

F.O.C.U.S.E.D

And I make room for expectation again.

Remind me that I'm not waiting alone—I'm waiting with You.

That the weight I feel is not meant to break me, Yet to build me.

That when the time is right, the promise will come—without flaws, without malfunction, without compromise.

Until then, I will trust the process,

Stand on Your Word,

And live like it's already done.

In Jesus' name, Amen.

F🌹.C.U.S.E.D

Affirmation: I Expect the Promise

I am not forgotten—God is still moving.

Even in silence, He's working behind the scenes.

The promise is still alive.

Delay is not denial. Preparation is not punishment.

I trust God's timeline, not just my own.

He's never late—He's always on purpose.

I am being developed, not denied.

This waiting season is strengthening me for what's coming.

I let go of fear and frustration.

I hold onto faith and expectation.

God is maturing the promise and maturing me.

When it comes, I'll be ready to carry it.

I live like it's already on the way—because it is.

I expect the promise. I prepare for it. I praise for it in advance.

Chapter 7: D – Discipline Over Distraction

"I discipline my body and keep it under control, lest after preaching to others I myself should be disqualified."

— 1 Corinthians 9:27 (ESV)

Focus doesn't just happen once. It's not a one-time prayer or a weekend breakthrough.

It's a lifestyle of discipline.

Discipline is the daily decision to guard your attention, your actions, and your alignment—especially when distractions are demanding more from you than ever before.

You can be called, anointed, chosen, and full of vision… Yet without discipline, you'll live off-center from the very thing God placed inside you.

Discipline Is What Keeps You Aligned

Discipline is the invisible structure that supports your purpose. It's not legalistic. It's not rigid. It's a spiritual boundary that keeps you from drifting back into old patterns that look familiar yet don't bear fruit.

Discipline says:

• I don't need to respond to every invitation.

• I don't need to entertain every thought.

• I don't need to chase every opportunity.

• I don't need to prove my worth to anyone.

Focus fades where discipline is absent.

Yet when you're disciplined, even distraction loses its power.

Distractions Will Always Be There

You won't outgrow distraction—you'll outtrain it.

It shows up in new forms: people, opinions, timelines, temptation, comparison, fatigue. Yet when you've built a life of discipline, you know how to respond.

Discipline doesn't eliminate temptation—it gives you the spiritual muscle to resist it.

It's the decision to:

• Say no when your flesh wants yes.

• Pray when you feel like scrolling.

• Rest when you feel the urge to overwork.

• Worship when you feel discouraged.

• Get up when you feel like quitting.

Discipline Doesn't Limit You—It Liberates You

A lack of discipline doesn't make space for freedom—it invites chaos.

Yet discipline leads to clarity, peace, and power.

The more you discipline your thoughts, the more clearly you hear God.

The more you discipline your time, the more fruitful your work becomes.

The more you discipline your emotions, the more secure your identity in Christ remains.

Discipline is the final key to staying **F.O.C.U.S.E.D**.

Ask Yourself:

• Where in my life do I need to reinforce discipline?

• What distractions keep pulling me away from spiritual alignment?

• What boundaries do I need to implement to protect my focus?

Discipline Doesn't Look Impressive—Yet It's Powerful

Discipline is rarely dramatic.

It won't go viral. It won't feel glamorous.

It often happens in quiet places—early mornings, hard boundaries, silent prayers.

Yet that's where the real growth happens. In the mundane. In the repetition. In the saying yes to God again and again and again.

Spiritual maturity often looks like quiet, steady obedience.

Because discipline doesn't just shape your habits—it shapes your heart.

And the more you practice it, the more
spiritually aligned, anchored, and available you become to the things of God.

 F.O.C.U.S.E.D

This Is the Call: Focus Is a Lifestyle

It's not about intensity—it's about consistency.

It's not about being perfect—it's about
being present and intentional.

The fruit of your faithfulness will be revealed over time.

And every small, quiet act of discipline is building something
eternal.

You are focused.

You are chosen.

You are aligned.

And with discipline, you will finish what God started in you.

When I Had to Step Back to Stay the Course

Discipline isn't always a straight path—it's a cycle of commitment.

There were seasons I stayed the course with clarity, strength, and
purpose.

And then… there were seasons I had to step back.

It wasn't because I was weak.

Yet because I was weary.

I thought staying disciplined meant never breaking rhythm.

Never missing a moment.

Never needing rest.

Yet I've learned that sometimes, the most spiritual thing I can do is hit pause.

To breathe.

To reflect.

To reset.

To regain my strength.

To sharpen my armor and my sword before going back into battle.

Because truthfully?

There came a point when I felt like my sword—the very thing I used to fight with—had grown dull.

I had served, prayed, fought, endured… until even my focus felt worn out.

And that's when God reminded me:

You're not called to be a machine.

You're not called to prove your discipline through burnout.

You're called to abide.

To rest and fight.

To reset and run.

To pull back when needed—so you can go forward with power.

So yes, I stepped back.

Several times.

And that's okay.

Because every time I returned, I came back stronger.

More anchored.

More intentional.

More aware of what truly matters.

Discipline isn't about perfection.

It's about getting back up—refocused and rearmed—every single time.

Prayer: When I Need to Stay Consistent

Father God,

Thank You for being faithful—even when I've been distracted.

Thank You for loving me through every detour, delay, and moment of doubt.

I don't just want moments of obedience—I want a lifestyle of alignment.

I want to live in a rhythm that reflects You—steady, intentional, focused.

Help me build habits that honor You.

Give me the grace to be consistent, even when I feel discouraged.

Help me to choose discipline over distraction, day after day, moment after moment.

I surrender my schedule, my emotions, and my impulses to You.

Train me to hear Your voice more clearly.

Strengthen me to resist the things that drain my spirit.

Center me in what matters most—Your Word, Your will, Your presence. When I feel tired, remind me why I started.

F.O.C.U.S.E.D

When I feel tempted, remind me what You promised.

When I feel like giving up, remind me that You finish what You start.

With discipline, I will protect my focus.

With obedience, I will pursue my purpose.

And with faith, I will fulfill the assignment You placed in my hands.

In Jesus' name, Amen.

Affirmation: I Choose Discipline Over Distraction

I am consistent, focused, and spiritually grounded.

I don't chase chaos—I choose clarity.

I protect what God gave me with spiritual discipline.

My purpose is too important to waste on distractions.

I don't need to prove myself—I need to obey.

I trust that daily faithfulness will produce divine fruit.

I show up even when I don't feel like it.

Discipline is my act of worship.

I resist what pulls me out of alignment.

God's presence is my priority.

I am building a life that reflects God's character.

Steady. Strong. Spirit-led.

I choose discipline—because I choose destiny.

Final Word to the Reader: Keep Choosing Focus

Dear Reader,

If you've made it this far, I want to say something simple, Yet true:

You didn't just read this book—you survived something to get here.

You pushed through mental clutter, emotional weight, spiritual fatigue… and you chose to fight for your focus.

And I want you to know—I see you.

More importantly, God sees you.

This journey hasn't been about perfection.

It's been about presence.

About choosing to show up for your life, your assignment, your relationship with God—day by day, step by step.

You've learned how to fix your eyes on the Father.

How to obey when it's uncomfortable.

How to cut out what doesn't serve your spirit.

How to understand your divine assignment.

How to stand firm when everything feels shaky.

How to expect the promise even when it's taking time.

And how to live with the kind of discipline that keeps you anchored through it all.

F..C.U.S.E.D

Let this book serve as your reset point any time life tries to overwhelm you again.

You're allowed to pause.

You're allowed to regroup.

Yet you're not going to quit.

You're going to stay F.O.C.U.S.E.D.

Because the world may keep shifting.

Yet your faith? Your focus?

That's between you and God.

Stay faithful. Stay aligned. Stay ready.

Your turn is coming—because your time is now.

With love and purpose,

Alainna L. Stephens

Closing Prayer: A Declaration of Focus

Father God,

Thank You for walking with me through this journey.

For speaking to me in the silence.

For reminding me of who I am and why I was created.

Help me to stay focused—not just for a moment, Yet for a lifetime.

Let my eyes remain fixed on You, even when life gets noisy.

Let my "yes" come quickly, even when obedience feels hard.

Let me release what no longer serves me, so I can make room for what does.

Help me to walk confidently in my assignment, even when I feel unqualified.

Teach me to stand strong when fear or doubt try to shake me.

Keep my heart expectant—because what You promised, You will perform.

And give me the discipline to show up for my destiny, every single day.

May I not just be inspired—Yet transformed.

May my focus lead to fruit.

F.O.C.U.S.E.D

And may my life be a reflection of Your glory.

From this moment forward,

*I am no longer distracted—I am **F.O.C.U.S.E.D**.*

In Jesus' name, Amen.

www.ingramcontent.com/pod-product-compliance
Lightning Source LLC
Chambersburg PA
CBHW020743130626
46554CB00006B/2123